Yes.

Yes.

Poems by Rosemary Griebel

*For Nina ~
In the shared
love of poetry!
Love,
Rosemary 2012.*

Frontenac House
Calgary, Alberta

Book and cover design: Epix Design
Cover Image: Brooke Lydecker - Getty Images
Author photo: Tasha Barrie

Library and Archives Canada Cataloguing in Publication

Griebel, Rosemary
Yes / Rosemary Griebel.

Poems.
ISBN 978-1-897181-49-2

I. Title.

PS8613.R53Y48 2010   C811'.6   C2010-906700-2

We acknowledge the support of the Canada Council for the Arts for our
publishing program. We also acknowledge the support of The Alberta
Foundation for the Arts.

Printed and bound in Canada
Published by Frontenac House Ltd.
1138 Frontenac Avenue S.W.
Calgary, Alberta, T2T 1B6, Canada
Tel: 403-245-2491 Fax: 403-245-2380
editor@frontenachouse.com   www.frontenachouse.com

for Richard
(Strong is your hold, O love)

CONTENTS

PART 3

I imagine that yes is the only living thing.
~ e.e. cummings

Part 1

MY FATHER COMES BACK

My father comes back as a draught horse
huge and shiny black. Muscles twitch and withers ripple
as snow swarms under street lamp, lights on his broad back.
His frame is made for hard work. Powerful hindquarters
and shaggy legs have memorized field and stone boat haul.
Iron hooves strike ground like a shovel.

How many nights have I looked into the darkness
remembering his fatigue, massive and silent as God's
on the sixth night. Exhaustion that comes
with building a new world, breaking hard land
to feed the generations that will come.

Perhaps my father has been in the garden all these years.
His head lowered to crop grass with the seasons,
waiting for me to come with a soft halter
and words bidding rest. His large white eyes
turned on a darkening world, cavernous nostrils
releasing ghosts into winter air.

HERE

Winter moon belly-up
over Fort Calgary. The homeless
huddled like smoke.

I once knew a homeless woman who said the night
was her mansion: every back alley,
and shallow ditch, a room.
Behind one door the smell of garbage and tar
behind another, sage brush and wolf willow.

And every room alive with sound:
the spit and rags of conversation,
cars chewing gravel, wind tossed in trees.
And that Christly racket, she said,
becomes the sweet hum of life.

The way stories can be stitched
into a single word.

But it's not the stitch of the story that matters.
It's the telling. And I think of my father,
an immigrant, traveling from farm to farm,
the weight of winter coming,
sleeping in hollows where the wind was small
catching him like a consonant.
And how he took those sounds
into his body: the bleached whispers of grass,
the murmur between stone and earth.

And how the land spoke to my father,
and said, *you belong,*
the way the earth speaks to the ones
begging on street corners, those curled
into hunger by the river,
their feet cradled by the soil,
a lover's hand.

And the land gave my father a new language,
so he could say:
coulee, chickadee, buffalo bean
the words, a map to his life.

And evenings when my father told stories,
his voice would become a well of deep water.

Sometimes he would tell the story
of Marconi, an Italian who traveled
to the shores of Newfoundland
and pulled the letter "s" from the sky
with a kite. A sound that traveled
all the way from England. All those words and letters
pitching through the air, connecting us.
And yet, Marconi sent a message home:
No words for this loneliness …

All those stories echoing, and knowing the past
is made bigger through the telling.

Sometimes when snow flutters like moths
around the window, I see my father,
a figure slipping like smoke into the dark sky,
the northern lights calling his name.

As if he was only one brilliant word.

BASHŌ VISITS THE PRAIRIE

He beholds
only emptiness.
It fixes his eye in its gaze
the way the River Ōi
clutches the moon.

There is nothing to write about
not even radishes.

Bashō's face bleached
as the cut end of a tree
as he tilts into the lilt
of the land, spring wind licking
the fish scent from his black robe.

Then comes the tenderness
after long looking.

Land once vague and blurred
opens with a moth white light
revealing red willow and silver sage
sun nodding on oat grass.

Perhaps a coyote, lurking.

STONES

In the spring of the sixth year
I was old enough to go into the fields
and pick rocks with my father.
Barefoot, I ran behind the stone boat
stopping only to stoop and gather.

As we piled rocks
by the fence line, my father
picked out a brown one
the size of a heart. It was imprinted
with the shadows of ferns
and trilobites.

Each stone, my father said,
contains the history of the world.

I still remember the hot green sun
the weight of the stone in my hand
the studded field opening
endless before us.

SUMMER, OUR BODIES

For Margo Harper

I.
Endless days when we were small with grass:
goldfinches flew through us, wild mustard scent,
pattering aspen. Texture of damp weedy runnels,
scrubby shrubs on distant hills shimmering.
Hand in hand through fields, the bleat and huff
of deer leaping beneath our skin.
The heart's saucer slopping over,
our bodies made of summer.

II.
Give us back blue, long-limbed afternoons
ditches rimmed with peppergrass, leaf hoppers,
two bicycles on a dusty road heading nowhere.

Give us back the slow lap of sloughs,
mud suck and brown skin of swimmers
wet grass running on bare feet.

Give us light from poplar trees, earth pouring
green, and everything in a fresh home –
moles, meadowlarks, cats with milky breath.

Give us two girls lying under barn rafters,
lift of swallows in the air, shimmer of muzzles
and motes, cool water from a deep well.

Give us black plowed nights for shaping
stories, knocking on dreams, entering them.
Bright words of constellations burning above.

III.
Rain falling on the dark city tonight,
the buried past rising like an invisible moon.
And somewhere deer leap though long grass
and girls swim green sloughs of memory.

Close your eyes. Summer still burns, saying, *here
I am.* All these long days I have been faithful.
All these long nights you are with me.

BISON

The quiet of bison,
mouths moving
over fescue
and milkweed,
sway of wind on throat latch
and bull's beard.

Dark, ancient ghosts
shifting over the land.

On this bleached prairie
salt flats beyond
Sullivan Lake,
the small light
of a torch
on a cave wall
at Lascaux
still gleams
in their wet, stone eyes.

LEARNING TO READ

For D, my grade one classmate

There was something about the light
around your pinched ears and stubbled head,
the sharp sky of winter holding
you in a rectangular pane
when you bent over the desk.

Words struggled from the dumbfounding book
like snared gophers in the tunnel of your mouth

look   *the*   *boy*

Sometimes I would will the text
from your lips, or whisper it into the open
before the teacher slapped out of you
dense traces of a code that wouldn't be broken.

We were so young then and had no understanding.

Though you were quick to hear

retard!   *bonehead!*   *calf fucker!*

By grade five you disappeared from school.

Sometimes I would see you in the fall
heading alone into the coulee with a gun
and an effortless eye for the spelling of the land.

Where words come from, where they go
how they pass from ink to voice
is still a mystery. Although in the sift
of memory, I recall the moment the page
opened up luminous, and the words lifted to me:

look   *boy*   *lost.*

NATURE I

Tonight, moth wings of snow
against the glass, black trees silent.
I'm thinking about everything that's dormant
within us. How the frankness of first love
falls away into another world. Long ago,
with crouched hearts we crept above
the sound of your parents' sadness
to your narrow room, polished agate
and arrow heads on the window sill. Outside,
the green of northern lights. *Shhhhh*. Listen.
In this place we adored not only the body,
but what rose from it: that fierce wonder of the land.
Love of snowy owls and horned larks, white weasel
in winter. Here, we remembered digging into
mouths of grass, small fists of fossil and fell,
original smell still on our skin. That night,
we were animals leaning against
the gates of the garden.

CLAM DIGGING IN THE BATTLE RIVER

That summer wild raspberries flamed
on the banks of the Battle River
as we blinded through murky waters
searching for clams. The air smelled of eternity,
the afternoon promised a life bigger than a town.

Filling a bucket with dark rocks of shell
we conjured the palpable curve of the future:
you would pilot a plane so high
the moon would be your sole companion,
and I would go west, skip words over the shifting light of water.

When you touched my hair I could not look at you
or the hungry mouth of sky. We gathered
buck brush and dried grass for the fire
as a hymn of mosquitoes hung above us.
The clams danced over white flames
until their reluctant shells surrendered.

Inside they were all muck and disappointment.

I gave the shells back to the sweep of water
as you called to me from the other shore.
The air that summer, full and sweet,
our lives certain as that ancient river.
Yes, that is what I remember best.

O youth. O you. O one. O none.

WILD CARTOGRAPHY

Tell me the landscape in which you live,
And I will tell you who you are.
  ~ Jose Ortega y Gassett

The loneliness that haunts you is of abandoned farms,
    earth and sky,
a black backbone of road.

The wind unfastens songs caught in the barbed
    wire fence, gives the earth no home.

Empty days waving above white fields,
    trees threaded by wind.

Whisper of cottonwood duff, velvet
    consonants of aspen at dawn.

Light perched on the horizon, waiting to drop
    heat on bluegrass and timothy
water kneeling in ditches.

Your body is a sweet vocabulary I discover
    one syllable at a time
bunchgrass, buckbrush, bulrush …
    this wild cartography of longing.

VERTIGO

There is the moment
    when you have the foretaste
        of falling,

there is the moment
    when you have the knowing
        and you leap.

We lay head to head
    under black trees, watching
        stars plunge

unable to speak
    because we had to think
        our way back

into the world.
    Somewhere out there loved ones
        moving in a lighted window ...

Yes, there was the warmth
    of touch and the smell
        of moist earth

but there was also that space
    between *then* and *now*
        and the foreknowledge
of after.

No one could find us
    and not even God
        was looking.

BE NOT FAR FROM ME

The milky way is a trapper's trail
across an empty sky,
the river holds geese
longing for the north.
In this landscape *hope*
is a small word. Ten years ago
we walked this dark river path together.
You said, *if you listen*
there is a kind of singing in things.

We held each other opening ourselves
to the night. New grass pushed against our skin
like wet tongues as our ears filled with sound.
Tonight your farewell note on the table.
This silence singing.

RECKLESS

Because we love most
the things we lose,
there is a recklessness.
It's why a man swims a deep river,
why he confuses fire with light.
And when the northern
wind comes hard
tethering winter darkness
to the heart
a man remembers a woman.
How she made him feel daring.
How when he was with her
it was the pull of treacherous waters.
Then this man no longer moves
through the day in the old ways
and even the lean light
of his wife's face
has lost its hold.
By the time cold is piled
against the door
he has forgotten the certitude
of the retreating shore.

HOW BRAVE THE BLACKNESS OF NIGHT

How brave the blackness of night
that marries aspen and owl
river and rock.

And with what certainty the field becomes
snow
surrendering shadow, surrendering light.

Tonight someone is writing a love story:
mystery, desire, redemption.
The writer knows not to use such words
for the sun is the reason
we cannot look at the sun.

What does it matter if you've left
without a good-bye? Remember the quiet
happiness of a room, the lover returned
from a long journey.

Let me be the patient earth, surrendering.
Let me be river, let me be rock.
Tonight there's nothing
I would not forgive.

MY MOTHER EXPERIENCES AN EPIPHANY
IN THE KITCHEN

Everything is radiant.
Walking from bedroom
to kitchen she feels the air
green with spring,
liquid song of meadowlarks,
grace of a new day.

And the light – the light shimmers,
illuminating ivory eggs in a blue
chipped bowl, earth brown potatoes
in a silver pail.

Beyond the kitchen window
calves bawl and bunt at teats,
robins tug at worms, meadowsweet pulls
at the golden light of the sun.

In that moment she recognizes
we begin and end as mouth:
greedily drinking at the breast at birth
death settling on the lips, entering
the mouth's shining bowl at the end.

And within my mother, cancer cells unknot.
Their small muzzles, reckless and radiant,
open wide to the soft giving in her body.

WHITE PELICANS

Huge and luminous in their arrival
that summer I spent evenings alone on the riverbank, the pelicans
swimming and scooping trout into their long, yellow-
orange bills. A flash of silver, a sluice of water
the fish twist and thrash against the smooth gullets.

The pelicans fed without a sound, their long necks
arched towards the water. I would watch
for hours, head down, eating my difficult grief.
I must have been comforted in the presence of
those prehistoric birds. Yet now all I remember
is the silence of swallowing.

WORDS, BURNING

Early morning, when everything is white
and frigid winds play ghost around the house.
A lone starling whistles down the chimney
as if to signal spring's thin retreat.
I don't want to remember farewells,
there's too much cold in the world.
I want to sit and think about my grandmother
humming as she kneaded bread, her snowy arms
moving like dancers, or lovers in a warm bed.
My grandmother, who did not believe in love
yet loved fiercely. I want to taste the burning of her words
as she told stories about far-away lands, and a dark man
lost to her. The way we lose loved ones, by something said –
or not said. The smell of rising bread and that light opening
    around her
the way the morning now opens around me. And I think of you
in a foreign land, all that should've been spoken.
Outside, the air brightens on aspen trunks
a lone starling whistles, and I write:
today, everything measured by distance –
spring, your words, this love.

THE PILGRIM

When you return from a long journey
air sweet with lilac and unfurled green
then you fall to your knees
and become gratitude's pilgrim.
You were given the way at birth.
Given blue fields and loam.
Given an open throat, wild orchids,
a path lit by milky stars.
You were given desire,
sweet darkness of the body,
white hum in the bone.

It's not the departure you long for,
nor the finish, with its thick incense,
tired feet and weeping.
It is the quiet loneliness in between.
When memory marries wind
and you are pure light. Walking.
One foot in front of the other.
You cannot speak of this place.
The way you cannot speak of grace
or what holds you to this world.
How at this moment you can only stand up
and move toward the light of home.

Part 2

❧

THREE WAYS OF SEEING HELEN KELLER

I.
Her first memory was light –
    The sun burning the room into clarity: white wicker
of cradle, a rocking chair in the corner,
    her mother's sewing basket gaping like
an open eye.

And there was sound –
    a dog barking in the distance, murmurs from the kitchen
below, squeak of floorboards. There was a taste for water,
    and her open hand was a fallow field of words.

Later, she remembers that when her mother lit a candle
    the darkness beyond was made deeper.

II.
Close your eyes. You may be surprised how easily the cup finds
    the lip, the sleeve finds the
            arm.
Limbs swimming through air, the railing curves to
    the hand, the stairs meet the foot.
Stop your ears. How quickly the body
    becomes sonar –
                flaxen texture of air when someone enters
the room.

Words that can be captured by caressing a throat.

In this white darkness the edges of the body hold the world
    the way a shore catches the ocean.

III.
When young Helen walked onto the stage she drew words
   from the air. Like a small gift, she turned sentences in her hand,
gave them to her help-mate, Annie.

And later, a woman from the audience recalled
   how it was as if light
was raining down upon Helen
   spilling onto her upturned face.

The whole world was alive behind her eyes,
   everything astonishing
      and awake.

Beyond the stage the amazed crowd watched in silence
   cowered in the darkness of something so bright.

HELEN IN FLORENCE

Smell, there is something of the fallen angel about it.
    ~Helen Keller

To touch Michelangelo's *David*
Helen leaves Annie at the foot
of the scaffold, climbs the colossal frame
until she can smell the cool
of his marble torso, stroke
the curve and dip of ivory ribs.
Some Florentines weep
when her hand moves like a skater
over the winter ponds of his eyes.

High above the crowd
fixing her body against David's strong arm
and the powerful fist ready for battle
Helen is overcome by a longing
stoked by aromas from a nearby kitchen –
the dark loamed secret of
truffles being shaved over pasta.
Inhaling wood-smoke and musk,
Helen becomes the earth-bitten ache
of desire which never says, *enough.*

That night Helen's dreams shimmy
with dissolute spores and fairy rings.
An infection at the scorched roots
of the hazelnut tree fingers its way upward
until the earth erupts, exposing
the wizened testicular globe of the truffle.

Awakening, hands warmed by inflections
of skin and bone, clutched scent of polished stone
Helen nostrils the empty air
holds the memory of *David*
the way absence holds desire
or the promise of something buried deep.

In the room below, Annie Sullivan
silvers open the gin bottle,
yearning for the intimate tongue
of juniper berry, the smell of raw nerve.
Touch me, Annie whispers, *just touch me.*

RUE GAY LUSSAC, 1978

Youth, a blue attic room in Paris,
where everything's an entryway –
new moon, hunger, the night

spooning rain on the cobblestone below.
Drunkards sing like soaked angels
while pigeons chorus from broken lintels.

On a broken bed that holds the dreams
of all the lovers gone before,
we listen for the yawn of early morning streets.

Stories shared like pieces of broken bread.

Faded backpack beside the door, rain
kissed from the mouth on a long night
in a room where we were astonished by love.

HOTEL ROOM, PARIS

That winter we lived in a room big enough
for a single bed, scarred table, a bowl
of plums on the window sill. And I read *Moby Dick*
over and over as the neighbours' tide of noisy sex
washed through the walls. *Gitanes* smoke
leaked under the door at night, curled up
with the naked light bulb over our bed.

Why after all these years do I come back
to that time? An age when I was an awkward force
moving through the world, bumping my head against
the history and traditions that bobbed above me,
thinking I could lose the Ahabs and Pequods
in a room that married all the strangers
who had been there before us.

Every one of us thought we were different. Handprints
on faded wall paper, neighbours tapping on thin veneer,
laughing, weeping. Hallways full of travelers and drunks
stammering their way to that single washroom
that held the intimate odour of piss and lilac.

Tonight, in my mind, I lean on a windowsill in that old hotel
with nothing but forgiveness for what haunts us,
for what we are driven to hunt down,
everything we must leave behind.
Beautiful, human desire. A handprint on a wall.
Someone making love, someone looking out toward
the bustling street, saying, *Look at this world. Just look at it.*

A NIGHT FULL OF RAIN

Winter, the heart visible in small ghosts of breath.
And here, a lit house on a dark Vancouver street,
the sycamore tree now bending over the gate.
Never more beautiful your face at the window.

Your face at the window, familiar as a winter moon
twenty years ago, on a night not this black.
And the rain? Never this wet or so filled with longing.
You said, through yearning we are given what we desire.

We are given what we desire through remembering.
Together in a night full of rain, how small we are.
Touching skin, knowing we are mostly water, bone.
If not for memory we would be lost to each other.

We would be lost to each other if not for this night.
When next clouds gather over this dark city –
please remember two lone figures at a table.
A sycamore tree in the rain, its bark white as bone.

THE MOUTH: A LOVE POEM

Mystery derived from Indo-European word meaning *closed lips; mute*

The way your silence holds a story
the ocean contains the changing moon.
And when I place my finger on your lips
I know I was drawn to salt-drenched words
holy sounds I had never tasted.

Tonight, loved one, I place my finger
upon the pale and leaven moon
knowing it's the unspoken stories
that fasten me to you
your mouth finding its way in the dark.

MYSTERY

I wish to write about things I do not understand.
~ Helen Keller

The way air holds
light, or the river
carries the weight of snow.
The spool of narrative
that reveals other ways
of seeing. The texture
of thunder and violets,
inconsolable gravity
of life. The difference
between geography and desire,
grace and prayer –
all the words in between.
The measure of passion
marrying the foot and the floor
the song and bull-black wine.
How sometimes when I think of him
I need the wall to stand.
The mystery of a stone or an orchid.
Silence, how it is its own language
        without being spoken.

THE LAMP

He is reading to his wife. How soft
the lick of flame in this room that smells of sod
and kerosene. Together they are a dark shadow
that bends toward the light.
She stares ahead, polished stone eyes.
He is reading about their son.
She leans in to listen but it is too dark.
So, she remembers how on the cot just there,
husband and wife would take turns
being field, being furrow. But that was long ago.
How does loss hasten so the night?
And now nothing but darkness.
The darkness, say, that's lurching
from her husband's mouth, his hand weeping
across the page, his voice
curling the lamp smoke.

JANUARY

It made no sense how she came home
taller that afternoon. He would wait
in the warmth of the kitchen,
everything made small by the cold.
Afternoon dusk lifted only by a yellow
school bus moving slowly along a white road.
He was just a friendly neighbour with hands
that had to tickle, play giggles
over small breasts, touch the nowhere
her shame invented. When she entered
the kitchen he knew she was bigger
than the blank brim of winter. It was the way
she walked into the room, purposeful
and dispassionate. The way snow
falls on bending grass.

IF INNOCENT

Traudl Junge was Hitler's personal secretary the final years of his life.

Some nights when it is dark
as a bunker, I think of you Frau Junge.
Your legs crossed, slim young fingers
typing his staccato words.
Yes, it was cold in that room.
He liked it cold as tundra.

I understand a woman, Frau Junge
wanting to please
a powerful old man, white God,
make him feel cared for,
make his words matter,
transcribing the beginning, the middle,
o world without end.

It could have been me
with a tender dusk of heart
witnessing the drab dress caught
on a chain link fence
the lone dogs sniffing an empty street
a piece of a mouth organ,
no mouth for it.

Rags of words. You were told:
Only the director is familiar with the play,
didn't question nervous whispers,
the stench over the city, slumped coat
in a mud field above your bunker.
The road so close.

I could have been you, Frau Junge,
haunted by dreams. Yes,
I have had those dreams:
Hitler, in the shape of a polar bear,
lumbering out of the darkness
Fur, coarse and yellow, soot-black skin,
blue tongue, teeth the size of fingers.

46

And you turn to me, Frau Junge,
your unblemished face and say:
Impossible. Our Fuhrer isn't a hunter
nor a meat eater.
Think of his modest appetite.
He only dines on clear soup
and smashed potatoes

THE PIGS

Maybe it was the way we became animals.
The rusty smell of turning meat on the grill,
the private urges of the bedroom, memory,
the summer heat and the women arriving
in his truck, night after night. The women
arriving with pink purses, thinking they were safe
from the street. And the pigs sleeping,
making those little noises that pigs make
when they sleep. Their velvet ears the size
of a man's hands. And what they can do.
The hands of one man.

Or maybe it was the season. Fall coming on
and that heavy light dragging across the land.
The details deepened the day.
We couldn't talk because there is no justice
when you know nothing is as it seems, nothing the same.

Remembering how as a teenager I fed pigs, an age
when the boys in big trucks talked about porking
the girls, and I loved their eyes. I loved the soft light
of the pigs' eyes when they looked up
from the trough. They trusted me to feed them,
would eat anything: fermenting grain, bones,
cabbage heads. Aren't we all born
into a trust with this world? And with what measure
and certitude do we get into sorrow's truck and ride.

AFTER FRANCO: THE SPANISH COUPLE

It was like a heavy quilt, the way the afternoon threw its heat over the hills. Together they slowly moved from bleached field to shade of trees, their clothes stained with sweat. There they drank water from a jug, ate hard bread, cecina and cheese. The leaves rustled in the small wind.

It was then they would talk between themselves. Sometimes about their children who lived in distant cities, or the work that needed to be done. Once, the husband recited Lorca's poem about the moon, and his wife wept.

They never spoke of what was buried in ditches or what the plow would accidentally leave under the hot sun.

Bleached bones
            surprised
by old death.

THE WAY OF THE WALL: JERUSALEM

Jerusalem stone is the only stone that can feel pain.
  ~ Yehuda Amichai

The way crevices are mortared with prayers
        slow and thick

The way the morning sun strays
        across creased lips

Petitioners weep, belief crouches within
        thirsty silence, a throat

The way blackbirds lift
        into warming air, burnt paper.

The way the body bends
        Hashem, who is like You?

JONAH SPEAKS OF THE WHALE

When they asked what it was like, I told them –
        Inside it was ocean, blue-black, and churning.
A barrel rolling away from land. My hand in front
        of me. Nothing but darkness.

When they asked what I heard, I said
        Voices. Someone calling my name.
Gurgling
        and guffawing.
God rowing past in a shaky boat.

When they asked what it smelled of, I said
        Warm brine. Sickness and vomit.
Cracked durian,
        baked in the sun.

When they asked if I was thirsty, I said
        No. What I drank tasted like breath.
Like lying down in the river, grey stones
        catching water, inhaling surprise.

When they asked how I passed the hours, I said
        I counted ribs. Each stave, a loved one left on land.
Memory of hands that smell of magnolia, heaven haunted
        light. The *shhh-shhh* that sounds like ocean,

When you're safe upon home shores.
        Memory of her holding me in her mouth.
Choosing not to spit me out.
        Holding me for love.

Part 3

SILENCE BROKEN

In response to Billy Collins' poem, "Silence"

You have muted everything in the room, Billy,
except the rain ticking on glass
restless and uninterested.
Now is the time to tell you what is on my mind.

Maybe you're expecting to hear
about the loneliness that is night
or the place called loss that looks
like an empty room.

I could tell you about a father
who walked miles behind a stone boat
turning the soil into plainsong, or a mother
who believed in the holiness of the alphabet,
companionship of the written word, the way

each of us comes to a poem listening
for perceptive words that will crack open
the meaning of this world. And yes,
I'm telling you this because

I believe a poem is the only way
to save life's silence
from being all it leaves behind.

Accompany me, and when I open
my mouth may the sloshing ocean,
deaf Beethoven, and the gods in their balloons
overhead, lean forward and inhale.

NATURE II

You remember the simple smell of dirt
while driving winter roads to Fort McMurray
where malls are overweight with stuffed shoppers
who cannot consume enough in this new Eden.
As a child you burrowed deep into leaf rot
and worm tunnel, inhaled darkness of badger and bone.

Paradise: earth, breath, sky above.
It was before you understood you were Adam, cast-out
into a world that had to be remade and renamed,
a new world, marked with hungry ghosts of gas wells,
methane skies, misshapen seasons, dirty brine
feeding the exhausted snow of winter.

Yet somewhere in you lives that green memory of a time
when the land lay down at night and listened to the moon,
carrots were sweet and orange on the tongue, poppies bloomed
the colour of summer. Everything was connected.
Ancestors wheeled among the galaxies, and earth was home.

TONIGHT

Tonight, no weight. The sun slants over
the city, air lifts and cools. Below the weir
cormorants form a black line, patient fishers
with a solemn duty. If I continue walking,
these lit houses, traffic, the glow
of office towers will become a dark blue
backdrop, and I will be in a field. The smell
of ripe timothy and brome. Owls calling.
I love this world. And I will wait here for you.

SPARROWS

God keeps his oath to sparrows
who of little love know how to starve.
  ~ Emily Dickinson

Do you think we long
for the charity of green fields
and thick forest?
No, our hearts' whir
is the flock swoop to concrete
towers and church spires.
Under bridges, over grey houses
we ride the long spine of day,
hop through back-alleys
where crumbs fall from
grubby hands and metal bins.
We are a scatter of *ifs* among
branches and battered leaves,
God's word in a world where everything
is rude, hungry and alive – not just
the pigweed cracking the back lot
but evenings at the shelter
measured out in prayer and song.
All of us small, moving with the wind.
Then gone.

LIBRARY

In the silence of the night when the living have left,
the whispers begin.

Penelope and Odysseus continue their yearning conversation
from the night they were reunited. Stalin and Hitler volley
insults across aisles, Sisyphus's bride bemoans hitching her life
to an old workaholic bugger.

Barbara Cartland is pushed up against Casanova,
Mahler is making moves on Moby.

On the children's floor, a skipping of rhymes,
huffing of wolves and frantic flight of fairies.

The books smell of Russia, of wood, of wet leaves.
They hold crayon scribblings, lost letters,
exclamations and whoops of marginalia.

In the basement at the bottom of the book chute
the Koran hurtles down and rests on the Bible.
The holy sing together.

As morning sun fingers across the shelves
the books are stilled, waiting like abandoned dogs
for the warmth of hands on their spines.

ON FIRST HEARING A RECORDING
OF VIRGINIA WOOLF

The winter I was seventeen I devoured all of your books
one after the other, and imagined your voice

like that of my mother's, traveling down a long hallway
from a room distant as childhood. You spoke of

the triumph, jingle and strange, high singing of life –
in its midst the feeling of being suspended above earth, alone.

Even then, I knew there were birds that flew by night,
though I couldn't see them or the land they left behind.

Every life is a kind of fiction, all longing, a dream. I turn the
    pages
and the lives of Mrs. Ramsay, Prue and Lily Briscoe follow.

Now, coming out of silence, echoey and static on an old
    recording –
your words with their plummy, ornate British tones, certain as

Bond street, girls in pink muslin, iron cooking pots and a
    lighthouse.
This sudden surge of tenderness: *Here you are, Virginia!*

Your voice intimate in my ears, your words which I have eaten
over and over so I could utter them, now alive in this room of my
    own.

THE STARRY MESSENGER

To look up at the Milky Way, its curdled knots of light
    and imagine Galileo staring at those same heavens.

How he determined the whitish band that spanned the night
    was not a nebulous cord, but brilliant stars in the millions.

The way you look at a huge, blurred scene and suddenly notice
    the particular – you are small as dust.

The fragile heart, the flimsy frame, cracked storm windows
    of the body. The long half-light of light that is a life.

Yet how you continue to not see things for looking –
    the slow peel of paint, the gradual downward arc

Of the spine. Even the love that is lit by a brazier of stars
    moves with the presumptive steadiness of a fixed planet.

Go out tonight and lay down in the sodden grass. Squinch
    your eyes, stare straight up into 15 billion years of life.

There among the strewings is old, blind Galileo appearing
    and reappearing like a star. He is waving

A white handkerchief from a great distance. You cannot hear
    him but his mouth is forming the words: Look! Look!

Feel the grass quicken, the edges of the field lift. Beneath, beside,
    above. You are surrounded by the world. And yet it moves.

GLASSES

There must have been a time when everything lifted
to my eyes with clarity: the new moon with the old
in its arms, white barley fields, my mother's hands.
Now I move through life mole-eyed, inward-looking.
Broken brush strokes of light and shape, details erased.

But with glasses: my alphabet, my understanding, more bright
and bright again. Circles of polished glass. O wonder.
And I remember thick-eyed Seneca who read all the books
in Rome by peering through a glass globe of water,
each murky word pulled from parchment, transferred
to memory's library, a hidden keep of knowledge.

Evenings, I stare bald eyed into darkness, watch
the lights of the city blink and disappear. One by one,
fellow dreamers remove their glasses, lay them aside,
welcome the dimming of the light. O bright soul,
together in the shelter of dark we go to the night river,
follow the small candles of the body, knowing, not seeing.

LATE NIGHT WITH PAIN

Fluorescent night, white hallways
fizzled fuse of ether and jaundiced limbs of the sick.

Pain tiptoes past, searches rooms where darkness
drips into veins, dribbles into plastic catheter bags.

Pain circles back, picks stringy meat of misery
from its teeth, checks the crinkled picture in its pocket.

Looks an awful lot like you.

     Hi sweetie!

Stitch of breath. Wince of weight on pulled tight linens.

Pain slips beneath the covers. Lifts your skin,
crouches between morphine and demerol.

     Listens.

Pain says I-I-I-I-I-I.

     Pain says boo
      hoo-hoo-hoo.

Ribs of blackness, anguished air.
Some wild, trembling thing within.

Morphine pushes out towards opaline light
thin heart flies along on a quivering string.

Pain winches it back, inches up the red filament
of spine. Fists each knobby protrusion.

Pain says, ask for cool water. I will drink it.
Pain says, think of loved ones. I will obliterate them.

Pain says, come. I will lift you into my little house.
              Set fire to it.
We have the whole night together
                         to feel it blister and burn.

THE BODY

To be at the stage in life when you think of the body
    as a weak vessel.
Vessel from latin *vascellum* "small jar or urn," also, "a ship."

When I visit you in the hospital, you are sucking oxygen
    like a cigarette
and studying the *Book of the Dead*.

The ward smells of washed limbs and disinfectant.
    Someone is moaning,
someone retching. Everything here is about the body.

Beneath cotton sheets you touch the soft dip in your belly –
    that hollow
where grief sits like a stone.

I wander down the hallway, peer into rooms where pillows
    are pinned down
with white flags of hair, the red doors of the body flaring.

In dreams, you are never old. You are on a ledge, and your father
    calls to you.
You do not jump because you love this life.

Read to me again. Read Bashō, the part where he says the body
    is composed of one hundred bones
and a spirit flimsy as a curtain.

The spirit in the vessel. You look up at me and your face
    is a strong, wooden prow.

And, oh, your fine body, with its muddling t-cells,
    swelling lymph nodes
and a nutmeg liver pulling the switches and levers of life.

Why this recklessness?

Let us sit together in this quiet port, in the washed-out light
    of TV, and pray your brave ship
not set sail on the tenth floor of this land-locked hospital.

FLIGHT

In memory of Grace Harvey

A yellowed copy of *Birds of North America*
among your few belongings
the pages hinged with brittle tape.

Inside a list of sightings with checks
and exclamation marks, the dates
small tracks of a life left behind.

The yellow wagtail, cinnamon teal and sage grouse
that delighted you
now narrowed to earth and bone.

When someone dies where does the love go?
Like breath and bird-song, into air.

Last night, snow fell like feathers
and I dreamt you returned from the dead
disappointed that angels can't fly.

Crippled with a too small wingspan,
sternum without keel, unable to dissipate
the heat of flight, they are metaphors of what remains.

In the end, you said, a hummingbird
is more a miracle of design than an angel
and you cannot bear all the beauty
that must abandon earth and air.

POEM WRITTEN BESIDE THE BOW RIVER

The winter you were so ill I would call,
listen to the phone emptying
in your house, worried you had walked
into deep river, the frozen moon
pooling in the shallows of your dress.
Undertow of darkness, gravity of silence.

What words can hold a life? Every spring
bodies are pulled from water into fresh sunlight:
the woman with dementia who confused a path,
a young man who leaves a bar and disappears,
a homeless woman who strides into a swaddle
of willow and ice.

Sometimes walking home along the drift
of dusky waters I pass the spirits who call the river
home – the ones who refuse to be retrieved by light.
I pick up a stone and write your name
and draw a picture of St. Francis.
The birds are in flight.

GONE

This is the world
without you:
the decanted light
of winter,
a rented house
on the riverbank,
your apple preserves
in the pantry
holding autumn
in a glass jar.

HELEN KELLER TO ANNE SULLIVAN MACY

In May 1905, Annie Sullivan, teacher, interpreter and devoted companion of 18 years, married Helen's editor and mutual friend, John Macy.

Annie, I imagine the moon pouring night over the back door as I push these words into the page. Did I ever tell you how paper feels like fire in my hands? Tonight, I could burn up a forest, my fingers, this stylus, these words, matches.

You with John, upstairs in our pine bed. The room where we woke the morning together. Swells and lulls. What pleasure we had finding each other in that dark cave of sleep.

What if I had said, *Don't?* He's my age, Annie. It's my words, my silence that brought him to our door.

The reporters will ask about the wedding. Say I cried with joy, my arms open to the day. If they ask about the future, tell them it is like the lake that rocks the boat safe to a shadowless shore.

Don't tell them I didn't want to let go of your hand. The guests milling about, creating that giddy air that makes everything smell white. I felt like the feral cat that ghosts through the house. Thin reminder of wildness no one wants to see.

Annie, last night I dreamt we were together in a red boat on Lake Pearl. The water lapped beneath us: *here gone, here gone.* The sheer happiness of being together. You spelled the light into my hand, and I held you with everything that has ever been true: words, water, the night. This love.

Stay, Annie, stay, Annie, go.

SUDDENLY THINKING OF HELEN WHILE
WALKING THE CITY AT DUSK

Shadowed voices and the purr of pigeons
from dark windows above.
Feel the *kashunk, kashunk, kashunk*
of tires on the bridge, sound
calibrated up the spine.
This moment – day dissolves into evening –
hinges become the door
office towers are night sky locked and shuttered inside.
The scent of wolf willow carried on cooling air.
The world enters through small gates.
Stars sweep past, river twists into
prairie, footsteps beneath the stones.
     Ghosts calling.
Come, take my hand.

(FOR WE ARE GOD'S HANDIWORK)

The ones who chase tornadoes.

The ones who set fire to their hair to prove hair doesn't burn.

Those who tie balloons to their lawn chairs to experience flight.
    And do.

The ones who have a reoccuring dream of writing a math exam,
    with no answers
        and no clothes.

Those who tattoo *dude* on their forehead. And forget the last
    letter.

Those whose hands don't tremble before they strike.

The ones who receive radio transmissions through their teeth,
    and hum along.

Those who go fishing to be alone, and end up divorced.

Some days even love feels provident.

Even for the ones who find the more they try to love people, the
    more they hate
        them.

And those who have decided to try *not to* love people, yet feel
    love lift
        like a lawn chair,
            borne impossibly into empty air.

GRETEL, THE LATER YEARS

Never mind what the books said:
the witch dead, Hansel and I returning
home to our cottage, step-mother and her dusky
heart, gone. The story didn't end there.

I developed a knack with spoons and oven.
From bright heat I draw shiny rounds of
bread, roasted partridge, sweet apple kuchen
its wrapping thin as parchment. Everything written

in the body, chewed over and over.
Early grief feeding remembered sorrow.
Brother and sister together, bent over bowls
mopping gravy, humming the thin tunes

that comforted us in the dark wood. Abandonment
now a kind of listening to which our bodies move.
No need to look to the forest, its dark distance.
Everything here in this room: beginnings and endings.

Outside, snow falls silent as bread crumbs on our small cottage.
The moon places its bones in the gate as I stir the fire,
take Hansel's plump fingers into my floured hands.
Our aging faces bend to the page: *Once upon a time …*

TELL ME

If you come back we will sit at the kitchen table
and drink glasses of dark wine. I will listen
to every word you utter. Your hands, birds that fly
the slipstream of memory. Tell me about the dream
where we pull your body from the water and dress
you in warm clothes. It is late and the dogs
are barking and no one can sleep. You are beautiful
and the milky way is a carpet we roll back towards dawn.
I didn't know the hollow bones of the heart break like small
    twigs.
Tell me about the weather. How the colours said *autumn*.
Purple fleabane and goldenrod, a street that smelled of ripe
    apples.
Go on from there. Tell me how everything was leaving:
wild geese, stripling winds, your house slumped towards ruin.
Tell me the mystery is not the light but how it passes through us.
How sorrow is like birds that lift, resettle and one day are gone.
You wanted to stay. Tell me that.

INSOMNIA

You may have heard this before – an ancient Egyptian
meditation called *quiet ears* can cure insomnia.
        You plug the ear canals with your thumbs
and listen for a high pitched singing in your head.
If you give yourself over to it, the sound will carry you
        into sleep.

        Outside, the moon is yawning over the city –
and the neighbour has arrived home. He opens a square of light
        to the night.

        My husband moves in his sleep,
pulls the blanket to his shoulders. He is curled up,
his ear pressed toward dreams. Now I understand how lovers
fly around each other night and day – how close and secret
        are the passages of love.

        Apparently that melodic sound
is always in the head – we just need to listen.
The way birds hear a choir of light, and in darkness
        start to sing.

Across the river, wolves in the zoo are howling.
        You may have heard this too –
imprisoned animals cry out for their kind, knowing
they are out there somewhere. All creatures
have an instinctive geography that goes beyond fences and cities.
        It is a map of belonging.

Even my own father would call out to my mother in the night.
        He could hear her walking above him in heaven,
opening doors, looking for him.

Right now the wolves are hearing things their keepers can not –
          the sound of jazz bars closing, the clock-tick
and night noises of humans: distressed crying, love making,
     and someone at a small window writing the world
while a distant keening in her head will not lead her back
          to sleep.

It is 3 a.m. I would like to wake my love so we could talk,
or lay our heads together like heavy hymn books, and listen.

WONDER

Here are the ones who wait in empty hallways.
The ones who watch time open and close the door.
The sky leans down, and a sun hard and yellow as tartar
Peeks in windows. No one wants to wake up.
Deep in the brain, a moth-like shadow.
The moth in mother that makes her forget.
Somewhere a photograph, and the slow heft of prayer.
Slippered feet and wool sweaters embroidered in flowers,
Lily of the valley and rose scent twined with catheters.
Soup, cream of. Biscuits and tea at three.
Out there, the pond's surface wrinkled with leaf tatter and wind.
The furrow and fluster fills the mouth with ash.
Creased maps of upturned palms, shawls heavy as wings.
To the quiet deepening, leave the silence to come.
To the young, leave the breadcrumbs of life.
This, the perfect emptiness that holds everything.

THE MONASTERY

I.
Here is a room built around silence
   in a house that venerates the word.

One window looks east
   and holds the morning sun.

One window looks west
   to field and rapturous wings.

The prayer in prairie, the scud and scuttle
   of sky. A leaf, a sheaf, paper white as milk.

Belladonna, angel's trumpet and a red poppy that sheds
   petals in the slow heat of afternoon.

Light of the sun, a yellow warbler sings. A yellow
   warbler is singing in the cottonwoods.

Who watered, who gathered, who weeded?
   Who is broken, who wept, who healed?

II.
In the musty light of a cellar, glass jars glow
   with crabapples and the sweetness of stinging bees.

A hot wind, a western wind that carries scent of
   cut grass and home, memory of another.

On this you come to me as a feral cat in long grass.
   On this you roll with the rollick of a garter snake.

I get down on my knees, and say, speak to me.

Sharp shinned hawks say ki-ki-ki. Whisper and hush
of foxtail, a black river of crows.

I get down on my knees, say, speak to me.

Summer wind replies: She loved you.

PLACES TO LOOK FOR A MOTHER

For Joan Shillington

After your mother's death
I wanted to tell you, grief
makes you a traveler
in the foreign territory
of everyday. Look for her
in small places: the pure loneliness
of early morning; the hollows
alongside animal trails leading
to salt; where the Milky
Way touches the darkness.

You will want to talk to her
as you fold empty clothes
into a garbage bag. Speak.
Later, the aroma of cloves
and you will be peeling
apples when she calls your name
through the clicks of a warming stove.
Listen. She is telling you
all that's gone is not lost.

WHAT IS HOLY

The white pages of a book.

The many ways a hand can open
   and close.

The brief darkness
   of a plane in front of the sun,
lives suspended overhead.

The way plants eat light –
   that is holy.

The endless voice of the ocean.

The streets of early morning
   when lone lights shine from the windows
of the elderly.

The eyes of someone who has lost love.

It is in the breath, and gathers into
   small sounds:
bread, home, yes.

When you bite into an apple and taste rain.
   That is.

WALKING WITH WALT WHITMAN THROUGH CALGARY'S EASTSIDE ON A WINTER DAY

Blue-white afternoon. The Bow river churns and smokes
as the city rumbles, economy chokes and bundled homeless
build cardboard homes in the snow. Yes, Walt, this is the new
world, and how often has your huge, burled form lengthened
beside me as we strode through parking lots, the filth and ice
of streets? Great seer, I listen for your relentless cheer
and barbaric yawp: *Unscrew the locks from the doors!*
Unscrew the doors themselves from their jambs!
The truth here is that it is not easy to loaf and invite
the soul when you fear death from winter winds; when crystal
meth is more common than a leaf of grass. But I am learning
from you. Today, when I passed one of the broken-down men,
I barked, *By God! You shall not go down! Hang your whole weight*
upon me. The man looked at me as when the pain is far away,
then suddenly clear. I kept walking (a small thrill of fear)
and summoned your great capacity for wonder as I headed
into the white, blurred fields where sparrows and homeless scatter
like chaff. There I quaffed the sharp chiseled air, the slow, sad light
of merciless winter and said, *yes, this world is for my mouth forever ...*
And I am in love with it.
Yes.

ACKNOWLEDGEMENTS AND NOTES

Grateful acknowledgement is made to the editors of the following magazines and publications where some of the poems first appeared:

Alberta Anthology: Winning entries from the 2006 CBC Alberta Anthology competition. Ed. A. G. Boss. Frontenac House, 2006; *Antigonish Review*; *Best Canadian Poetry in English*, 2010. Ed. Lorna Crozier. Tightrope Books, 2010; CBC Radio's *Alberta Anthology* (2001, 2006); *CV2*; *filling Station* (first prize winner, "Inner Poet" contest); *FreeFall Magazine* (first prize winner in Freefall Contest, 2009, 2008; second prize winner 2003); *Grain*; *Home and Away: Alberta's Finest Poets Muse on the Meaning of Home*. Ed. Dymphny Dronyk and Angela Kublik. House of Blue Skies, 2009; Three chapbooks published by Leaf Press. Ed. Patrick Lane; *Malahat Review*; *Prairie Poetry*; *Room of One's Own*; Take the Poetry Route (ETS buses and LRT); *Writing the Land: Alberta Through Its Poets*. Ed. Dymphny Dronyk and Angela Kublik. House of Blue Skies, 2007.

Writing this book has been a rich journey and I was fortunate to have many steadfast guides along the way. Often I turned to the writing of earlier masters including Matsuo Bashō and Walt Whitman. The Bashō quotes are taken from *Narrow Road to the Interior and Other Writings*, translated by Sam Hamill (Shambhala Classics, 1998). The Whitman quotes are taken from *Walt Whitman: Poetry and Prose* (The Library of America, 1996).

I drew inspiration and valuable information from Dorothy Hermann's *Helen Keller* (Alfred A. Knopf, 1998), while writing the Helen poems.

Billy Collins has written more than one poem titled "Silence". My poem, "Silence Broken" is a response to Collins' poem "Silence" which first appeared in his collection, *Picnic, Lightning* (University of Pittsburgh Press, 1998).

I am indebted to the friendship and support of fellow writers in Calgary's "Thursday Poetry Group" including Joan Shillington, Robert Stallworthy, Juleta Severson-Baker, Chris Dodd, Frances Hern, Cassy Welburn, Garda Robinson, Micheline Maylor, Cort Delano and the many, many other fine writers who have been at the table sharing poems and contributing to the discussions.

What we listen for in poetry is a way of being in the world, a way of knowing. I am particularly grateful to Patrick Lane for teaching me to listen and helping me trust the wisdom of the words. He is my contemporary Bashō.

And to Richard Harrison, who edited this book, and has been a master guide from the very beginning, my love and profound gratitude for showing me the way.

Finally, to my husband and family, thank you for being the *yes* in my life.